HORSEPOWER

HOT RODS

by Sarah L. Schuette

Reading Consultant:
Barbara J. Fox
Reading Specialist
North Carolina State University

Content Consultant:
Butch Patrico, President
Michigan Hot Rod Association
Detroit, Michigan

Capstone
press®

Mankato, Minnesota

Blazers is published by Capstone Press,
151 Good Counsel Drive, P.O. Box 669, Mankato, Minnesota 56002.
www.capstonepress.com

Library of Congress Cataloging-in-Publication Data
Schuette, Sarah L., 1976–
Hot rods / by Sarah L. Schuette.
    p. cm.—(Blazers. Horesepower)
    Summary: "Describes hot rods, their main features, and how they are
built"—Provided by publisher.
    Includes bibliographical references and index.
    ISBN–13: 978-0-7368-6781-8 (hardcover)
    ISBN–10: 0-7368-6781-3 (hardcover)
    1. Hot rods—Juvenile literature. I. Title. II. Series.
  TL236.3.S336 2007
  629.228'6—dc22   2006023661

Editorial Credits
Aaron Sautter, editor; Jason Knudson, set designer; Patrick Dentinger,
    book designer; Jo Miller, photo researcher/photo editor

Photo Credits
Corbis/Richard A. Cooke, 26–27
Index Stock Imagery/Image Port, 4–5
Photo by Ted Pappacena/www.dragracingimagery.com, 24–25
Photos by Ron Ceridono, 6 (both), 7, 8–9
Ron Kimball Stock/Ron Kimball, 12, 13, 14–15, 16–17, 18–19,
    20–21, 22–23, 28–29
SuperStock/Brian Lawrence, 10–11
ZUMA Press/Robert King, cover

The author dedicates this book to her father, Willmar Schuette, and
his 1946 Chevrolet Suburban.

1 2 3 4 5 6 12 11 10 09 08 07

TABLE OF CONTENTS

MAKING A HOT ROD

Watch this old car turn into a hot rod. Chop the top. Pull off the wheels. Remove the old engine. Then patch and sand the body.

The car is ready for a new paint job. First, the primer is sprayed on. Then the body is painted candy-apple red. A new engine and big tires are added next.

Finally, put in new seats
and add lots of chrome. This
hot rod is ready to roll.

BLAZER FACT

Owners often use parts from other old cars in their hot rods.

CUSTOM CARS

Big tires, slick paint, and shiny chrome give hot rods lots of personality. Sometimes flames or pinstripes are added too. No two hot rods are exactly the same.

Hot rod owners might lower
or chop down the car's roof. They
add short windows to help create
a sleek look.

Some hot rods sit close to the ground. Owners lower frames or change suspensions so the body sits lower. This process is called channeling.

Fenders and running boards may be taken off or changed. Finished hot rods are sleek and smooth.

BLAZER FACT

Any car or truck built before 1949 with a changed engine or body can be a hot rod.

ENGINE POWER

Hot rods rumble down roads with large, powerful engines. Owners sometimes replace original engines with powerful V-8s for extra speed.

Blower

Blowers force extra air into a hot rod's engine to boost its horsepower. Large blowers sit above the hood. Small blowers are hidden under the hood.

BLAZER FACT

Blowers are also called superchargers. Blowers mix more air into the fuel to make cars faster and more powerful.

HOT ROD PARTS

Blower

Engine

Suspension

Short window

Streamlined body

Exhaust

Big rear tire

23

SHOWING OFF

People used to drive their hot rods in drag races. Now faster cars have taken the place of hot rods.

Today, hot rod owners cruise all over the country. Roaring engines, glittering chrome, and snazzy paint let owners show off their cars.

BLAZER FACT

Hot rod owners often hunt for and share hard to find parts at swap meets and car shows.

ONE MEAN ROADSTER!

GLOSSARY

blower (BLOW-ur)—a device that mixes more air with fuel in an engine to create more power

channeling (CHAN-uhl-ing)—a method of lowering a car so that the body is close to the ground

chrome (KROHM)—a coating that gives objects a shiny, metallic appearance

fender (FEN-dur)—a cover over a car's wheel that protects the car's body against damage from stones and reduces splashing

horsepower (HORSS-pow-ur)—a unit for measuring an engine's power

primer (PRY-mur)—a base coat of paint that goes on before the main color

suspension (suh-SPEN-shuhn)—a system of springs and shock absorbers on a car or truck

READ MORE

Braun, Eric. *Hot Rods.* Motor Mania. Minneapolis: Lerner, 2007.

Corbett, David. *A History of Cars.* From Past to Present. Milwaukee: Gareth Stevens, 2006.

Nielsen, L. Michelle. *Vintage Cars.* Automania! New York: Crabtree, 2006.

INTERNET SITES

FactHound offers a safe, fun way to find Internet sites related to this book. All of the sites on FactHound have been researched by our staff.

Here's how:
1. Visit *www.facthound.com*
2. Choose your grade level.
3. Type in this book ID **0736867813** for age-appropriate sites. You may also browse subjects by clicking on letters, or by clicking on pictures and words.
4. Click on the **Fetch It** button.

FactHound will fetch the best sites for you!

INDEX